THE MATTER OF MATTER

THE MATTER OF MATTER

DEJAN STOJANOVIĆ

NAB

New Avenue Books

NOTE TO THIS EDITION

The poems in this collection are part of a series titled *The Embrace of Light and Darkness,* marking their first publication in book form. The collection includes poems originally written in English between 2005 and 2010, with a few exceptions that were added or fixed later.

D. S.

Contents

BRAIN-UNIVERSE

SPIDER

The day justifies itself through the memories it promises.

Roses hold the secret of a scent unknown to them.

Lovers are often happy captives of sad illusions.

Children long for knowledge and beauty

That may not seem so lovely once discovered.

Nothing will be lost, but nothing will be saved either.

The future is as real as the past, yet the present does not exist.

Memory without a touch of sorrow is like food without spices.

The mind is both a hunter and the hunted.

There is no punishment because there is no true death.

We are enslaved more by our illusions than by our desires.

It is not the human being, but their mind stumbles over a rock.

The tireless spider weaves countless traps,

But the ultimate victim of its net is the spider itself.

SHAKESPEARE'S SOUL

Lightening thoughts shine in visions,
About life and everything under the stars.
Dreams that others do not dare to dream,
Streaming directly from the Source of Light,

Feed the soul nurtured by the natural rhythm of the heart
That hardly any computing algorithm can match.
Machines can organize words into sentences,
 Yet they do not have emotions that can create true art.

Even though machines can outsmart people in computing,
They do not possess the refinement of the human soul to be
     creative
But under the lead of humans and their creative nature
No height or goal is unachievable.

Machines can outsmart the human brain in many areas
But only human hearts can create true art.

BRAIN-UNIVERSE

The entire World exists within the human brain.
With 89 billion neurons and 100 trillion connections
Between them, along with 30 trillion cells in the human body,
Each one of us holds the Universe within.

Explore the vast interstellar regions of your imagination.

Thoughts are messages traveling between neuro-galaxies.
We are both the marvel of the Universe and the Universe itself.
Our thoughts and feelings shape the World we perceive
As well as the World that exists beyond our senses.

Recognize the wonders and answers you discover within.

A challenge arising from profound truths
Often goes unnoticed, even after we find an answer,
Yet, even without the answers, we believe that the ultimate
    secret
Lies in primordial nothingness filled with divine potential.

Your intuition will lead you more wisely than any textbook.

Cherish the miracle of being alive,

And the even more remarkable miracle of universal existence.

Embrace the wellspring of your imagination,

The force that unites the entire world.

Take a moment to look up and talk to the stars.

RESCUING HIDDEN THOUGHTS

Unlock the thoughts that lie dormant within words,
With art that brings life to ideas.

Uncover the hidden gems that await
In unexplored territories beyond language.

Embrace the adventure and discover
The miraculous worlds that reside within!

It's not you who is adrift;
It's your thoughts that feel isolated.

Invisible truths quietly illuminate
The minds willing to perceive the unseen.

Like the forces that support the Universe,
Profound thoughts patiently wait

For a brave explorer with the courage to dive
Into the wilderness and reveal their essence.

WORDS AND THOUGHTS

We need either a new language
Or a fresh way of thinking.
We have grown tired of empty words.

The problem lies not in the words themselves
Or in our experience, but in the speed
At which we reproduce them,
Compounded by deception.

Avoid using gimmicks to attract
New readers, clients, voters, or customers;
Refrain from relying on effects and showmanship;
Remove the "Sale" sign from words.

One authentic idea is worth more
Than an entire book filled with well-worn,
Stale knowledge and information.

THE MAGIC KEY

Some people navigate the world with confidence,
Yet they can get lost in a forest of thoughts.

Others may wander through life,
But find stability through their mental strength.

Some possess keys for many doors,
Yet they often end up in unwelcoming places.

Others never misplace their keys
But still feel lost in their experiences.

Some frequently lose their keys,
Yet navigate life with unwavering certainty.

Meanwhile, others don't need any magical keys
To explore the world and the rich depths of their souls.

LITTLE FAMILY

The World grew from a small dream,
Which blossomed into a massive tree,
With roots deeply anchored in the original dream,
Sustaining itself with the knowledge gained from it.

From a small dream, great hope emerges,
Spreading its roots across the sky,
Nourished by the wisdom acquired through dreaming.
A little family of dreamers shares the common vision.

Knowledge is less important than the life
Of a dream that supports those
In pursuit of forgotten truths.
A small family deciphers the ancient dream.

The sole purpose of the knowledge
From the original small dream is to nourish
The family of dreamers who long to uncover it.
Those who dream of knowledge embody knowledge itself.

In life, two dreams converge;
The knowledge of one becomes the essence of the other,
Yet, the dream remains unified.

Both sides are equally ineffective without each other.

One needs more knowledge to unravel the secret,
Yet knowledge is lifeless without the dream.

THE TRUTH INVISIBLY SHINES

The truth shines invisibly through silent sounds.
Help wisdom find you.

Don't go anywhere unless it is your own decision.
Be cautious of free advice.

Do not cling to unverified truths;
They are often less reliable than dreams.

Don't waste time complaining when faced with challenges—
A little more effort is all you need.

When you feel pressured from all sides,
Be determined enough to persevere

In order to reach the place you have always been,
Even if you weren't aware of it.

Freedom is not a matter of chance,
It is a matter of merit.

LONELY STONE

It is unwise to hoard all the knowledge you have acquired;
It is far more rewarding to uncover
Fragments of an immense treasure—
Joyful, tempting, challenging and fleeting.

The World is a solitary stone in limitless space.
Life flows like a river—
Meandering through existence
With knowledge as its only companion.

Understanding is akin to a solitary stone;
It is knowledge personified.
You are the witness, and you, too,
Are the knowledge, the river, and the stone.

ELOQUENT PSYCHOPATH

There is a new creature in the jungle—

An eloquent monkey.

He has lost much of his hair,

And appears slick and polished,

Dressed in expensive suits,

He always smiles, revealing his bright white teeth,

He enjoys reading, especially dictionaries;

He is charming and seductive,

Plays golf, and attends important events,

Mingling with many influential people.

You can spot him wherever cameras are present.

He makes promises, both possible and impossible,

He wakes up early because his schedule is always full.

His admirers often become his first victims,

Yet nobody realizes that he is

A new and dangerous creature in the jungle.

FREEDOM

One more discovery, and everything will be resolved.
But what should we do with all this freedom
If the secret lies only in a new patent
From an accountant turned scientist?
This expert understands the intricacies of the stock market,
Currency exchange, money supply,
The Federal Reserve, debts, mortgages,
Sub-mortgages, financing, and emerging trends.

This accountant-turned-scientist
Has now become known as a sophisticated investor;
His concern is for the well-being of free individuals
And the nations he proudly guides
Toward a state of absolute freedom for all.

This speculator labeled a sophisticated investor,
Pretends to lack knowledge—not about freedom
Or inventions, but about the illusion he creates.
He offers a lifeline to all who do not know
What to do with their newfound freedom.

THE MUSEUM OF WAX FIGURES

THE MUSEUM OF WAX FIGURES

He told us he would build a new society,
And then he left.
Another came
Promising to rebuild the old society,
But he, too, departed.

One followed after him,
And yet another,
Each making grand promises
To rectify past mistakes,
Only to leave as well.

The entire gallery of figures
Fills the Museum of Wax Faces,
Staring at us with the truth,
While we are left to manage the work
That remains after they have gone.

POETRY AND REALITY

Poetry is a translation of silent conversations

We have with the World,

Conveying emotions that transcend

What language can truly express.

It captures the essence of dreams

And the truths hidden within them.

Poetry is a beautiful illusion

That is larger than reality.

It serves as a meeting place for souls,

Which shine as the true homes of creativity.

Poetry cannot be found solely in music or rhythm;

Those are just vehicles for it.

Poetry is life painted in more bearable colors—

A truth that doesn't suffocate with self-righteousness.

It embodies both philosophy and something beyond it;

It is a science more precise than science itself.

Its nourishment comes directly from the ultimate source—

Poetry is the food, the air, the earth, both new and old;

Its message is understandable, even when it appears obscure.

Poetry is weary and seeks fresh perspectives,

Exploring new emotions

To create new pathways for communication.

It doesn't require excessive baggage

If its purpose remains clear,

Whether on paper or in the digital world.

Poetry no longer needs to rely on rhymes;

It doesn't have to be remembered

Through the repetition of refrains

But instead, through the recurrence of light.

POEMS

Some poems are a joy to read,

While others provoke deep reflection.

Some help us discover ourselves,

While others find us unexpectedly.

Some are hidden away,

While others remain open and clear.

The best poems don't explicitly teach us;

Even when they do, they invite us to look beyond language

To access a deeper source of knowledge

That many people already understand.

This understanding is felt rather than articulated—

Experienced in the gut rather than through words.

Some poems are like spells,

While others resemble stories.

Some are like volcanoes,

Seemingly feeding the fountains of paradise.

Some poems are pure sounds,

While others embody the essence of poetry itself.

Some poems are a joy to read,

And some inspire deep reflection.

Some we discover, and some find us.

Some are hidden away,

While others remain open and clear.

SUMMER BY THE SEA

The sea gently pulses,
Carrying the sweet scent of summer
To the city bathed in the glow
Of streetlamps. The music is loud.

Women move gracefully,
Their alluring fragrances blending
With the aroma of summer in the city.

Confusion builds and intensifies
As summer sweeps over the sea,
Filling this vibrant and cheerful place.

Untamed desires immerse themselves in the froth
Of summer's magic force,
Pulling them deeper into the night.

The music grows louder,
And you know how it goes
When the ghostly summer wind
Draws everyone into the bubbling pot of heated cravings.

SUMMER AND WINTER

Summer or winter depends on our mood,

On the music we listen to,

On the city we inhabit and the people around us,

On our connection to the sky,

On the memories we recall from our travels

Through various towns and landscapes,

Through the tranquility of an oasis,

Through the chaos of our thoughts,

Through wild nights and dreams.

Summer or winter, spring or fall—

These are not just the seasons

But the states of our minds.

(LOST) HISTORY

The interpretation of events often obscures history

With fragments of taste and peculiarities

Captured by historians, rulers, and sycophants alike.

The truth can be beguiling and distant despite our efforts.

What truly matters is not the accuracy

Of the truth or the falsehood itself,

But the motivations behind each narrative.

An unyielding life shapes these motivations,

Compelling individuals to accept an imposed truth

Rather than navigate the barren landscape

Of lost and silenced history.

MAGICAL BOX

Even when we travel far away,
We never truly leave behind the familiar places and faces.
They linger over the snowy mountaintops,
Bringing with them the scent of linden trees,
Accompanied by the lights of houses that resemble stars,
Scattered just enough along the roads at night.
We watched these lights through the window
As our parents drove us toward new experiences,
From which we remember only the glow.

A faithful friend follows us wherever we go—a magical box
Full of essential items and various treasures.
It holds fragrances, ornaments, scars, and a few grains of wisdom.
From this box, we occasionally pull out memories:
An almost forgotten spring,
A flower given to an unknown lady,
An old, adorned drinking fountain near the park
In the city we once called home;
The music that still plays from within the box,
And the eyes that once captivated us.

There are cafés, streetlamps, and little springs
Where we drank water along the way

To the sea—a destination we eagerly awaited every year.

All of this continues to live on in the magical box,

As the little Sun shines over the picturesque landscapes

Awakening almost forgotten sounds and memories.

If we seem to lose these memories,

They never lose us; they linger and eventually find us,

Whether we are in a desert

Or deep in the heart of a jungle.

We can still hear the music from the magical box—

Fountains in the desert garden.

Even when we travel far away,

The magical box remains,

Pulling us back without warning.

CLICHÉS

I was eager to share

The most important thing with her,

But it felt like a cliché.

The words shouted in my head,

Yet even that felt cliché as well.

I tried to come up with something better,

Only to find myself stuck in another cliché.

I shook my head, closed my eyes, and prayed—

Once again, it was cliché upon cliché.

Finally, a tear slipped from my eye,

And she understood,

Even though a tear is a cliché too.

YOU ARE HOPE

When I speak the truth,
You claim it is a judgment rather than the truth.
When I share white lies,
You say they are just fantasies.
When I try to express something
I can't fully articulate,
You say I am simply rambling.
When I speak to share,
You tell me I talk too much.

Yet, I keep trying to convey
What I need to share—
Something that I can't repeat endlessly,
So, I cover it with words and fantasies,
Because if I attempted to express the real meaning
Of what I truly want to say without words,
It would strip away all its significance.

THE GREATEST ARTISTS AND SCIENTISTS

The first pioneers spoke,
Trailblazers who sketched the first curves of the alphabet,
Bravely ventured into the unknown,
Building bridges of language and awakening dormant minds.

Yet often, the most significant pioneers—
The unseen visionaries and silent heroes—
Fade into the shadows, their names lost to time,
Frozen on the silent lips of history.

In the tumult of past events, they remain overlooked—
Unrecognized giants, part of the silent
Collective genius of humanity
Shining like invisible stars hidden by darkness.

Without their courage, where would we be today?
Each letter and every word serves as a testament to their legacy.

WAITING ROOM

WAITING ROOM

A terrifying scream or a gentle whisper,
Waiting in the dark.

A troubling thought,
Wrapped in the velvety fabric of language.

An omen of boredom,
Lurking in the mud.

Bliss in the vacuum
Of the waiting room,

Where a flower grows.

THE UNKNOWN

Apparitions, clouds, and fog;
Unknown faces in unfamiliar places
That somehow feel familiar.

Unknown shapes and elements,
Unknown feelings and thoughts
Have strangely become familiar.

Unknown sciences, teachings, and laws,
Obscure figures and undiscovered teachers
In some way feel familiar.

An unknown past, present, and future
Lived without understanding,
Yet still feel familiar.

Even you, unknown to yourself,
Wonder and gaze at a world
Designed to feel familiar.

THE SHADOW OF DEATH

What is it that follows you
Like a shadow not cast by light?

Inside your being,
It lingers.

An invisible shadow,
Stronger than life.

A shadow living within a shadow,
An animal without teeth,

Biting slowly into a shadowy realm,
With the patience of a predator.

Bloodthirsty patience
That promises eternal life.

SOME OBJECTS OF ART

Even the overlooked object
Fights for its place.

It has survived many bruises,
Living on through its scars.

It was the labor, disguised as love,
That gave it life.

Still, it cries out,
Drawing attention to its scars.

Lame and sterile,
Yet, it yearns for vitality.

Hungrily and jealously, it moves
Through the crowds of other objects.

It spreads a silent message:
"Look at me; beauty is boring."

CONTAMINATED MINDS

Born from despair,

They become magnets for disaster.

Eager for attention,

They create situations just to be noticed.

Thriving on misery,

They poison and dilute joy.

Although they claim to cure madness,

They only produce more chaos.

They multiply at an alarming rate,

Abundant yet easily spread.

Emerging from broken hearts,

They act like invisible, incurable viruses.

Their goal is to find a place in others' hearts

To form a large, contaminated family,

Born from their despair.

NEW MAN

Fly toward the inner sky to reach the outer sky.

Consider the Moon merely a first station.

Listen to the emptiness to find your way.

Travel through memory to discover the future.

Learn from the distance that touches the horizon,

From which the mountain grows, splitting the sky into two.

Be that mountain, embracing new planets and territories.

Domesticate places whose names you do not know.

Name the future after yourself.

Give birth to the grassy fields

Of the new landscapes you create and cultivate.

Define reality and the gap between yourself and the world.

Rename the sky and the Universe.

Offer enchantments and songs to every piece of ground you enrich.

Conceive a new language more powerful than one made of words.

Think, sing, and communicate without words or music.

Make the world sing and talk to you.

Become a listener of spheres,

A listener of waves traveling through space,

A listener of unheard music.

Become an angel whose wings guard the edges of your garden.

Bring with you all your knowledge, history, and heritage.

Build a new family stemming from the old one.

Bring discoveries, artefacts, songs, and books—

Bring it all and share it widely.

Offer gifts ranging from roses to diamonds

Or whatever you have,

For the Ultimate Lady—Existence.

Charm her with all your spells;

To win her heart, you must earn her trust.

Do not be too shy around her.

Share everything you know, even your secret plans and mischief.

She will listen to you,

Even when you speak something outrageous.

Once you find a place in her heart,

Your entire journey will be etched there,

And you will uncover the true meaning of your experience.

GREATNESS

You become a slave to anything you hoard.

Unchain yourself from the burdens of ownership;

By doing so, you become the true master of yourself,

Which is the most valuable possession in the Universe.

Vanity acts as an emotional scarecrow, driving people away.

Do not feel diminished by your insignificance.

Avoid striving for greatness solely for the sake of being great,

Unless it serves the purpose of helping others.

Help others recognize their value.

By assisting them, you become a part of their lives.

You become more of yourself

When you allow others to be themselves.

There is no greatness greater than the wisdom

Gained from modesty in the presence

Of the magnificent Universe of which you are a part.

Yet, you remain yourself, enriched by the whole world.

BONFIRE LOG

I willingly give you my heart,
Which you turned into a bonfire log
To warm your cold soul.

THE WAY

Nothing grows outward;
It only grows inward.
The way out is within.

You are both the traveler and the Path.
There is no you outside of yourself.
(You are your own Path.)

CRYSTALS OF FIRE

POOR UTTERANCES

Aim to speak more thoughtfully,
But don't hold back
When your voice truly needs to be heard.

If you choose to wait
For a moment of significance or a pivotal event,
Remember that it may not arrive as you hope.

What could be more valuable than the beauty
That comes from your desire to articulate your feelings,
Before they fade into silence?

You can convey your emotions and needs
Without resorting to outbursts, tears, pleas,
Or using less effective words.

LION AND ZEBRA

The zebra runs alongside other zebras,

Galloping with a trembling heart.

Her black-and-white stripes

This time attract death.

Bewilderment fills her as dust swirls around,

But it's all in vain; she cannot escape.

The lion's gaze cannot be deceived,

For what it sees is neither black nor white,

But red.

DNA AND BEAUTY

Would there be beauty without color?
Would all the shapes blend
Into an unrecognizable mass?

What is beauty?
Is it defined by the richness of color,
Or perhaps by shape, sound, or smell?

The dilemma remains: is beauty deserved,
Or is it merely a random consequence
Of accidental causes and events?

There would be no beauty
Without a universal algorithm that creates it,
Shaping and reshaping all
That flows through the DNA.

MESSAGES

Waves are messages

Sent into space.

They are not just forms of energy;

Instead, they encompass the entirety of knowledge

From both the past and the future.

Yet, they overflow with freedom,

Unbound by determinism.

An entire infinity exists

Within a small message, confined

In immeasurable space

Beyond our comprehension.

This reality is shaped by the freedom

That thrives within the determinism

Of an undetermined infinity,

Rich with inexhaustible possibilities.

UNIVERSAL BATTLE

Without conflict, nothing holds true meaning.
Even in love, differing elements clash.
Everything is at odds with everything else,
Creating a constant struggle—even during times of peace.
These periods serve as moments for rest and recovery.

Most often, the battles we face are not intentional;
Rather, they arise from a struggle between energies
Striving to survive and find harmony.
We aim to crystallize our understanding
Through constant examination,
Sifting through excess and eliminating
What does not contribute to our idea of progress.

This pursuit leads to breakthroughs
That grant us freedom from the constraints of instincts,
Outdated beliefs, and the burdens
Imposed by biology, history, and geography.

CRYSTALS OF FIRE

Flowery Sun,
Without fragrance,
Gives birth to flowers of emptiness.

From its hot heart,
Sunny petals grow,
Explosively majestic.

His Majesty—the Sun,
Her Majesty—the Flower,
Two in one—one in two.

Lustrous petals—crystals of fire,
Dancing with the planets,
Warming the cold and lonely night.

WHERE DID THEY GO

All the people who still live in our memories—
Where have they gone?
Memories rush into oblivion,
Filled with battles and friendships.
All the loves, tragedies, and histories—
Dead stars and alien civilizations fade away—
Just like the summers spent by the sea
That once felt so real and enduring.

CHOOSE WHAT SILENCE CHOOSES

Love me not for what I have done;
That is merely an act of courage.

Love me not for what I have learned;
That is simply knowledge.

Love me not for what I have said;
That is just talent—
A skill or a moment of sincerity.

Love me not for any obvious reason;
That is just a reason.

Instead, love me for what I have never said—
For what silence chooses to reveal,
For what only silence truly understands.

MAN-MADE GOD

Horses gallop,
Red, white, black, and pale.
Thunderous mountains rise
With divine words in visions—
Stronger than words or swords,
Stronger than emperors or reason.
Enslaved by reality,
In which believers dwell,
A man created a nightmarish God
In his own image.

CONQUERORS

They will come again; they always do.
This time, they will be more articulate and polished.
They won't just take; they will also give.
They will be more dangerous.

Nobody will recognize them.
No one will know where they come from
Or what they truly want.
They will arrive as friends—
Generous and welcoming.

Instead of taking gold,
They will bring gold, silver, and money.
They possess it all.
There is still something they do not own: You.
This time, they will come for your soul.

A FLOWER IN EMPTINESS

FAKE AVANT-GARDE

If we all claimed to know everything,
Nobody would truly understand anything.

The right to beauty stems from genuine knowledge,
Embraced by an anarchist dilettante
Who proclaimed the right of ugliness
To exist as ugliness
And the right of ugliness
To also be beautiful.

Who decided and declared
The different types of beauty and knowledge—
Ugly beauty or beautiful ugliness—
A flower without a scent,
Burnt petals, muddy colors,
Iron spikes instead of thorns,
Blooming in their democratic right.

Ugliness seeks an easier path to beauty,
But beauty had to pay a hefty price to earn its place
In the hierarchy of valued ideals.

SAYING IT WITHOUT SAYING IT

Tricky words can obscure true meaning.

Genuine feelings often express themselves through what remains.

If a single word could encapsulate love,

It might not convey much value.

Wrapped within a small, unspoken sentiment,

True meaning can communicate without the need for words.

The essence of the world can be contained

Within a single, unexpressed feeling.

The core of life often resides

In the simplest, one-syllable expressions.

Even if feelings are left unspoken,

Their true significance can still resonate.

Instead of relying on words,

Let your actions illuminate and enlighten the world.

LOVE EQUATION

I am fading away inside you,

While you thrive within me.

As I perish, my love deepens;

The flower of death embraces life.

In dying, I discover life—

A vibrant force that nourishes passionate love.

You are a river, a sky in my thoughts.

I swim through the currents in my veins,

Striving to reach the sky.

In dying, I am blossoming;

In living, you warm my life,

Nurtured by your love.

BOILING POT

It requires more energy to hate than to love.

Hate has to invent reasons,

Similar to water in the desert

Of a thirsty mind.

It is a boiling pot

Ready to explode

At anyone who hates to hate.

FLOWER IN EMPTINESS

It's not just the words that go unsaid;

It's the events, the experiences, the mysteries.

It's not the music that remains unwritten;

It's the whispers of the Universe.

It's not the feelings that cry;

It's the love that faded from love.

It's not death that waits;

It's life in disguise.

It's not memory that is lost;

It's the rebirth of the known in the unknown.

It's not the vicious cycle of life;

It's the circle of possibilities.

It's not the repetition of what is possible;

It's the rendition of the impossible.

It's not merely what is possible;

It's the infinite nature of the impossible.

It is the cosmic Flower in emptiness,

Growing from nowhere into nowhere.

CASTLES

How difficult it is to touch the horizon,
To see the other side of reality.
We dream of dreams, endlessly dreaming,

Inside the castle where the secret library is hidden,
Within the womb of a dream, in the embrace of a ghost.
This castle grows within us, revealing

What we cannot see, yet still
Offering glimpses of all the dreams
Stored in the books of a library we seek.

We dream on the road toward the castle,
In a labyrinth filled with birds, animals,
Insects, plants, planets, stars, galaxies, and universes.

We yearn for new light, new vision,
A new touch in a more harmonious world,
As we gaze upon the brightest light of flight.

Walking through this very dream,
Unique among all in the vast labyrinth,
We are the castles we are searching for.

PARKS AND STREETS

While he walks down the street, he thinks of other streets—
Perhaps one in Florence, Paris, or New York.
He reflects on the beauty yet to be discovered
And continues to walk, dream, and ponder.

Parks embody a universal quality;
They are tranquil oases
Set apart from the noisy surroundings—
A true heaven in the urban jungle.
Though cities differ greatly,
All parks share a similar essence.

In one park, he encountered a love
He had lost in another park.
To get from one park to the next,
He had to traverse various streets.
These streets spanned different time zones,
Yet all the parks occupied the same temporal space.

He began to feel diminished
And started moving faster through the streets,
Which began to blend into a single avenue.

It was neither the Champs-Élysées nor Boulevard Saint-Michel,

Nor was it Park Avenue or Fifth Avenue.

It was not Michigan Avenue in Chicago,

Avenida 9 de Julio in Buenos Aires,

Piazza del Popolo or Piazza Venezia in Rome,

Palazzo della Signoria in Florence,

Campo dei Santi Giovanni e Paolo in Venice,

Corso Vittorio Emanuele II in Milan,

Parliament Street in Exeter, England,

Prince Michael Street in Belgrade,

Or Red Square in Moscow.

It was a blend of all these avenues,

Leading him to the park he discovered

While he wasn't actively searching for it.

He found it as he walked down a street he thought he did not like,

Evoking strange thoughts in unfamiliar lands.

CHURCH ON THE HILL

There is a Church on the hill
In which no one ever prays.

Or perhaps you are the Church
To which you direct your prayers,

Trying to climb unknown hills,
Deciphering dreamlike visions.

God is searching for you,
But you are a runaway.

THE SECRET OF THE WHOLE ONE

I am real, even though I am not.

Such a sweet contradiction:

To be the one who exists

And yet the one who does not.

I soared to the depths of emptiness

And kissed the light

With the lips of darkness, and I returned

While remaining in the same place.

When you are, you are not,

And when you are not, you are.

That is the secret of the Whole One,

Which is and is not.

OUTCAST

The Earth is a round dream, and the Sun is another.
Both exist side by side in the vast expanse of the Universe.
Roundness dances upon itself while flatness stretches out,
Creating distance—a newly formed space and a fresh dimension.
The horizon extends far, lost in its infinity.

The Sun remains, and the Earth stands fixed.
There is no revolution, no rotation,
Yet, the Sun circles the Earth, and the Earth orbits the Sun,
Together, they journey through the Milky Way,
While our galaxy spins around a central black hole,
Its majestic, invisible light glows deep within.

Where do flatness and roundness meet?
What lies at the heart of circularity within this hollow sphere?

In this circle of emptiness, a phantom atom struggles,
Seeking its place in the vast nothingness.
Space is not merely space; it is a void,
Seduced by its own curves, encircling a hollow sphere,
Wrapped in layers of emptiness.
This creates a relentless cycle of circularity, being, and non-being.

ABOUT THE AUTHOR

Dejan Stojanović (1959) was born in Peć, Kosovo (formerly part of Serbia, Yugoslavia). Although he received a legal education, he has never practiced law. Instead, he became a journalist and foreign correspondent in the early 1990s; however, he is primarily a poet, essayist, philosopher, and businessman.

He has published the following poetry collections:

Circling (Krugovanje), Narodna knjiga—Alfa, Belgrade, published in three editions: 1993, 1998, and 2000.
The Sun Watches Itself (Sunce sebe gleda), NIP Književna reč, Belgrade, 1999.
The Sign and Its Children (Znak i njegova deca), Prosveta, Belgrade, 2000.
The Creator (Tvoritelj), Narodna knjiga, Belgrade, 2000.
The Shape (Oblik), Gramatik, Podgorica, 2000.

The Dance of Time (Ples vremena), Konras, Belgrade, 2007.

Pentalogy: *The World in Nowherness (Svet u nigdini),* Udruženje književnika Srbije, Belgrade, 2017:
(1) *Ozar (Ozar),*
(2) *The World and God (Svet i Bog),*
(3) *The World in Nowhereness (Svet u nigdini),*
(4) *The World and Humans (Svet i ljudi),*
(5) *The Home of Light (Dom svetlosti).*

The Hidden Light (Skrivena svetlost), Čigoja, Belgrade, 2018.
Primordial Spark (Iskra iskona), Albatros plus, Belgrade, 2021.
Centuries and Steps (Vekovi i koraci), Albatros plus, Belgrade, 2023.

Essays:

Creator and Creating (Stvaralac i stvaranje), Albatros plus, Belgrade, 2021.

The New Man and the New World (Novočovek i novosvet), Rad, Belgrade, 2022.

Anthology: *Selected Serbian Plays* (*Izabrane srpske drame*), USA, 2016.

A book of his selected interviews, *Conversations* (*Razgovori*), was published in 1999 by NIP Književna reč in Belgrade. The Serbian Heritage Foundation and the Association of Writers of Serbia for Intellectual Engagement awarded the book the Rastko Petrović Prize.

Collected Poems: 1978-2000 (Pentalogy 1), New Avenue Books, 2025 (Translation from Serbian).

Books written in English:

Philosophy: *Absolute,* New Avenue Books, USA, 2024.

Poetry Series: *The Embrace of Light and Darkness* (Pentalogy 3):
- *Dance of Sounds*, New Avenue Books, 2025
- *The Matter of Matter*, New Avenue Books, 2025
- *The Home of the World*, New Avenue Books, 2025
- *All Women in One*, New Avenue Books, 2025
- *Strange Thoughts* (prose), New Avenue Books, 2025

He lived in Chicago, USA, from 1990 to 2014, and holds citizenship in both Serbia and the United States.

www.ingramcontent.com/pod-product-compliance
Lightning Source LLC
LaVergne TN
LVHW041325080426
835513LV00008B/602